anthroprose

also by jennifer pirecki
reckoning with dust

praise for reckoning with dust

"In *Reckoning With Dust*, Jennifer Pirecki has the courage to actually believe that we are made in the image of God and just a little lower than the angels. She tackles head on what it means to be human and by transference, what it must mean to be God, while creating a greater sense of awe and inspiration for having taken the reader on its gritty journey. There is a gaping hole in literature that *Dust* fills."

~ Monty Powell, BMI, ASCAP and SESAC award winning songwriter, author of *A Guitar and a Pen: Stories by Country Music's Greatest Songwriters*

"I constantly search for scriptural reflections that strive to be more honest than novel, more earthy than relevant. Jennifer Pirecki's *Reckoning With Dust* both surprised and stirred me. The short entries lend themselves well to the lost art of ruminating—chewing and chewing again on the absolute flesh and blood of the biblical characters, and the incarnated Christ running through the middle of them all."

~ John Blase, Editor, Penguin Random House, poet and author of *The Jubilee, Know When To Hold 'Em: The High Stakes Game of Fatherhood*

"By examining the personal dynamics of Jesus and those who knew him, Jennifer Pirecki's *Reckoning With Dust* explores humanity's universal struggles. Retold with much care, love and insight, *Reckoning*'s stories help connect what she has learned from the actualized Jesus and the sacred terrain of her clients' experiences, while serving as a guide to understanding our own relationships and our own selves better."

~ Danan Whiddon, healing educator, herbalist and author of *7-Day Gratitude Challenge, Emergency Gratitude Practice for Broken Hearts* and *Educational Experiences: Student Essays*

anthroprose

jennifer pirecki

redfern ink
franklin, tennesee

anthroprose copyright © 2019 by Jennifer Pirecki.
All rights reserved. No part of this book may be used,
reproduced or transmitted in any manner without
written permission from the publisher, except in the
case of reprints in the context of reviews.

Published by
Redfern Ink
P.O. Box 15
Franklin, Tennessee 37065

Cover design by Design9Studios

Printed in the United States of America.

www.jenniferpirecki.com

ISBN: 978-0-9994690-1-9

Library of Congress Control Number: 2018959824

for Bekah

for Zoya

help us
live through
our own reckonings

jennifer pirecki

hold
true
to who
we are meant to

anthroprose

what is at stake?

I am

jennifer pirecki

can you see his scars?

You will relearn
to walk
and in due course
you will relearn
your Self

jennifer pirecki

will your fear overtake you
and keep you
from knowing me?

the only way I know he is True
he knows everything about me

while they retreat
he remains
with kindness and warmth
like I have never known

somehow it seems he understands

jennifer pirecki

> you have persevered
> through much
> I am here to gather you up
> and help you
> set things a right

anthroprose

how I long for you
to share
in my joy

jennifer pirecki

but
buried deep
resides yearning
for a
life
liberated

anthroprose

it is still with me
this ache

jennifer pirecki

he seemed
to come
from a far off place

a familiar stranger

anthroprose

as always
you rise

jennifer pirecki

>
> the caves
> my scribes
> their walls
> my scrolls
> their symbols
> my language
>
>
> in their cool hovels
> I would hear
> whispers

anthroprose

her drawing inward has worn them out

jennifer pirecki

the essence of suffering
when we need most
we are left to face
what only we must face
there is no one else
not even you

anthroprose

none pierce the isolation that has become like skin

jennifer pirecki

loving intention
does not quench
the longing

his pain
his want to hold on
his will's refusal
to be shattered

my body breaks

jennifer pirecki

family
and friends
hover

tethered
though
disconnected

anthroprose

stand
silent
witness

jennifer pirecki

betrayal
from a brother
who knows me
taught to expect it

nonetheless
it has crushed me

to follow calling
I risked rejection

jennifer pirecki

this
intimacy
unsettles

they
don't know how
to make sense
of it

more tenderness shown
would unravel them

anthroprose

they
are too busy
puffing up
vying
for favor

jennifer pirecki

your touch
reminds me
not to depart

stay present
a little longer

anthroprose

care nothing
for their glowering

jennifer pirecki

you know firsthand
what I need

I will try
to recover something
of a life
after losing you

I will never forget

jennifer pirecki

I have no energy
for shortsighted wonderings

I need steadfastness
some courage

there is
no hesitation
in your sweeping movements

jennifer pirecki

wash away the heaviness
so I can catch my breath

anthroprose

they have always envied our closeness

jennifer pirecki

your eyes catch mine
filled with longing
and gratitude

the brewing storm
beneath
your familiar serenity

you hold my soul
take it to your death
and whatever comes after

jennifer pirecki

our friendship is my most cherished treasure

there is a silent agreement between us

jennifer pirecki

      this extravagance
      a sacrifice

anthroprose

sorrow presses me
to your feet
I slowly unfold
from my collapse

your departure
falls on me
like suffocating blackness

another
will never fill the void

jennifer pirecki

    the turning tide
    will scatter us

    terror
    dread upon dread
    for knowing
    much less loving

    conserve your strength

you have been my anchor
it is my turn to be yours

jennifer pirecki

      kindred spirit
      friend
      how can I let you go?

I see it in your eyes
your gaze lingers
then you are gone
sights fixed

jennifer pirecki

I will try to trust
what you have said

you will be with me
in other ways

as you traverse the depths
I pray my gift
will hold momentary relief

jennifer pirecki

> they are dear
> however frustrating

shallow breath
chest heaving

anguish eases
with every touch

jennifer pirecki

to surrender proves difficult

anthroprose

you are family of my heart
respite from the strain

jennifer pirecki

> I hold dear
> our times together
> our walks
> our conversations
>
> I will always remember

anthroprose

I feel your agony
I do not want to leave you
you have grounded me

jennifer pirecki

at this threshold
to my darkest hour
I will carry your presence

anthroprose

enduring this season
exacted a surprising toll

jennifer pirecki

she
can hardly face me
without
breaking apart

she knows

with
your shattered body
breaks my heart
you carry a piece

it
will crush you
as it will me

jennifer pirecki

the bough breaks
the sparrow falls

just beyond my grasp

heart open
hand extended

jennifer pirecki

your twisted vision
keeps you from seeing

you grip too tightly
your emptiness

scraping yields a fraction

jennifer pirecki

until that moment
until your very last breath
even beyond

there is still time

you think
you are
the only one?

such is the path
of all

jennifer pirecki

to the still
small voice
that cries out
within you
listen

anthroprose

you believed the lie
of your victim

your truth
can overcome

jennifer pirecki

to be fulfilled
too daunting
too unknown

anthroprose

be fulfilled

jennifer pirecki

you are not the first
nor the last

anthroprose

it is not too late
even for you
it need not end

the knowledge of
what could have been
will crush you

as it will me

anthroprose

I have found the tree that will serve me well

jennifer pirecki

      meager to some
      thirty pieces of anything
      is more
      than I have seen in a lifetime

      a lost inheritance found

anthroprose

I didn't know then
what I know now

no amount
would satisfy this ache

jennifer pirecki

numb the hunger for a moment

anthroprose

I have thrown in
with the darkness
that haunted me
I can no longer outrun it

it has caught me
I am traitor

jennifer pirecki

ravenous
the runt
the number of us
the only thing that flourished

a tribe
yes
a tribe of ne'er-do-wells
also yes

the lack haunted
so tired
from wanting

jennifer pirecki

one might say
my upbringing
brought with it
a necessary creativity

how I long
for the days
of my walkabout life
to take me away
from this drama

jennifer pirecki

you encumber yourself with regret
mistake it for motivation
or some lack to overcome

it is just your way

anthroprose

friend
to this day
and beyond

jennifer pirecki

    we run together now
    I in you
    you in me
    we are one

anthroprose

I wanted you
to know what
our connection
made capable

jennifer pirecki

your guilt
will be left behind

it is not needed
where you are going

anthroprose

you choose
a posture of remorse
to face down
the dust of your origins

jennifer pirecki

I saw your stalwart nature
your hunger for meaning

there may be a cost
unintended
lasting
consequence

will your fear overtake you?

jennifer pirecki

do it in secret
this scheme
that is what I told myself

anthroprose

it is a privilege
to know what I know
and see what I see
and travel this path

jennifer pirecki

she knows without yet knowing

anthroprose

my mind's eye sees

jennifer pirecki

       these people know me
       and have known me
       but cannot stretch
       to see me

anthroprose

speak the truth
without hesitation

jennifer pirecki

>she is fearless
>let the record show
>the surety of her

anthroprose

to be awake
is to take stock
of what is against

jennifer pirecki

change within is difficult

at
the heart
of this life's struggle
holding Truth
through daily practice

jennifer pirecki

like moth to flame
I am drawn to
his wisdom

his soul is ancient
yet he speaks of
young mind
young mind
always the children

what could this mean?

in quiet whispers
you may hear me
or you may not
almost silent
I stalk
I haunt
'prey
listen'

you retort
'not now
I am too busy
with this or that'

jennifer pirecki

they cannot see
beyond her uncleanliness

she has suffered enough

to feel clean
to wear a fresh garment
these are the stuff of fantasy

jennifer pirecki

    new waters call you
    swim with their current

who is this persistent soul?

ah
there she is
I knew it was a woman

jennifer pirecki

he saw in me
what I could not

anthroprose

how does one bait a hook to catch a man?

jennifer pirecki

am I too old to understand?

you know
there are others
who will not travel this path

perhaps
even those you
dearly love

this devastates you

jennifer pirecki

he tells me his secret
how can it be?

it is hope beyond hope

I stand at the edge
of my abyss

and you taunt me

jennifer pirecki

formation of fingerprints
came second
to my wiry grip

muscle before flesh
cunning before consciousness

this life is welcome misery

I am sent
to the river's edge
disrupting solitude
my arrival startles
our struggle ensues

he has wrestled with life
more
than he has done anything

he will not go quietly

jennifer pirecki

I see you
disillusioned
stretched
to the brink of breaking

this must end
so that your future can unfold

anthroprose

a new name
a gift

he will see
no benefit in that now

jennifer pirecki

your days of deceit have come to a close

your body will give way

a foreshadowing
of what would have been
without my intervention

jennifer pirecki

>
> his reflexes are primal
> his strength at its apex
> each maneuver reveals his skill
> honed by years of gamesmanship
> at home and abroad
>
> he will not go quietly

his body stiffened
housing untended anger
sealed by young trauma
grown old
inside of him

jennifer pirecki

his memory
holds frozen
rage-filled images
these mix
with his fermenting shame

it seems
there are no answers
for my condition

the prodding and concoctions
of various healers
have accomplished nothing

save to line their pockets
with whatever I could pay

jennifer pirecki

you have persevered
through much
there is still time

anthroprose

there is still time

jennifer pirecki

stolen are the years
with my beloved
absorbed
by youthful longing
unfulfilled

anthroprose

you think YourSelf a stronger foe?

jennifer pirecki

these deceits ravage me
twenty years
are as the day
of my swindling

I linger
I am here
to gather you up
and help you
set things a right

jennifer pirecki

it only requires
Love's tending
to flourish
your seed of goodness

anthroprose

it only requires Love's tending

jennifer pirecki

>it
>only
>requires
>Love's
>tending

it is their pattern
their habit
meant to be challenged
by you

this
your mission
your time

jennifer pirecki

the sins
of your father's father
set this in motion

lineage of neglect
left you
to feed your darkness
untended

jennifer pirecki

they would forget to remember

where is the justice?
were my days a trifle?
you have wiped the ledger clean

what do I have to show for it?

jennifer pirecki

you mistake sacrifice for scarcity

after all
he could have refused
to walk the path
before him

jennifer pirecki

I have lived within the confines of frailty

anthroprose

I feel alone
at the edge
of this deep

even you have
abandoned me
so it seems

jennifer pirecki

wearing shame like
her tattered tunic
she cloaks herself

to hide
elude

if this meaninglessness prevails
what matters?

you
could never
bear the fate
of a vagrant wanderer

you
haven't
the stomach for it

jennifer pirecki

he saw in me
what I could not see
and bathed me
in his knowing water

anthroprose

I could not see
what he saw in me

jennifer pirecki

I was bored
craved a new challenge

convinced
destined
resigned
none would find me
in this backwater place

I would never amount to much

he is unmistakable
even from a distance
I wish I could run to him

I will crawl

jennifer pirecki

vulnerable but sturdy

you are mine
you are loved
you are not forgotten

jennifer pirecki

I barely allow myself
this seed of hope
that something
of another place
roiled through me

bumbler that I was
saying the wrong thing
at the wrong time
wavering in my belief

jennifer pirecki

rough hewn he found me
a miserable excuse
too serious
brooding
my griping would repel

there was never enough to speak of

tuck me
in the folds
of your garment

you mistake
sacrifice for scarcity

this
is why you need rebirth
to shed your fear
share your secret

jennifer pirecki

long ago
I made peace
with my loneliness
to keep it
from devouring me

besides
it has become
my only comfort

kindred
you have done well
to fulfill your part

forerunning
in life
and in death

jennifer pirecki

I wonder
how I contribute

my success too often
one step
from my defeat

the brush
of your hair
brings me back
from the abyss
that yawns before me

jennifer pirecki

these are times you walk the knife's blade

to dust
she returned

from dust
she transformed

jennifer pirecki

    I remember
    I am your dream

anthroprose

he lacks flexibility

jennifer pirecki

flesh-on-bone
give me something
not elusive talk
or impossible concepts

anthroprose

flourish
in the meantime

jennifer pirecki

throw off the cloak of guilt

speak
without
hesitation

anthroprose

there are days when all I can see is my failure

jennifer pirecki

this dream
of a memory
is all I have

I wish
I could hold on to it

you think your Self
too weak for
the loneliness

make peace with it soon
life is riddled with it

jennifer pirecki

she has been passed over long enough

to heal the essence
of one
is worth more
than one hundred
cures

jennifer pirecki

distraction
is often
chosen

stillness
instead

I do not fit
within their timing
they feel
they should have known
sooner

jennifer pirecki

I must leave
release them to their fate
as I am released to my own

there are others
who will see

anthroprose

they must reduce me
to a previous version
of myself
to satisfy

jennifer pirecki

you are not forgotten

living through
would deplete
his reserves
he would
pull from
something deeper
to endure

jennifer pirecki

wash away the heaviness

remove the gritty remains
from my dusty journey

blinded
often by impulse
uncertainty
or hardship

they would forget
to remember

jennifer pirecki

I see
what they do not
her untapped brilliance
the brightness
her sorrow veils

anthroprose

I am the mirror
reflecting
their failure
to see clearly

jennifer pirecki

there
is no way around
only through

this
is the beginning

I can sympathize now
it is effort
to stay clear and connected
when there is rejection
and there is always that

jennifer pirecki

catch my breath
concentrate
soles of my feet
feeling their way
steadying the pace

anthroprose

to be awake
is
to take stock
of
what is against

jennifer pirecki

no help
can be given
if I am not
within my Self

she is formidable
she can see right
through me

jennifer pirecki

he remains
with kindness
and warmth
like I have never known

his voice
lacks the judgment
of the others

somehow
he understands

jennifer pirecki

her determination
reminds me
of my mother's will

anthroprose

from every pore
confidence oozes

glory days

jennifer pirecki

would others approach me
in the face of scrutiny

craving some diversion
from the emptiness
that consumes us

jennifer pirecki

you have bitten hard
on the hook set for you
you took the bait
when you were ready

shed your fear
share your secret

jennifer pirecki

none could know
the full nature
of my quest

anthroprose

I am seeking
the center
of your soul's stage

jennifer pirecki

your fire will be used for other things

anthroprose

he is not lost
this prodigal

he is weary

jennifer pirecki

>let my dark corners be
>is that too much to ask?

his light
would carve
and sear its way
inside

scorning me
all the while

jennifer pirecki

>
> my
> purpose
> is
> Beyond
> and
> Within

anthroprose

remember your grandmother's embrace

jennifer pirecki

what
would it
be like
to walk
and
move
without
this
nightmare?

anthroprose

my heartless taskmaster
ever my companion

jennifer pirecki

you have until
your last breath
even beyond that

it is not too late

anthroprose

the prayer of her blood has been answered

jennifer pirecki

she is fearless
she has gathered her power back
now she can rest

anthroprose

I visit him
in the shadows
of the night
it is not wise
to be seen

jennifer pirecki

I steady myself
I am at the mercy
of what is to come

I grow weary
he must get on with his journey

one last blow
unwinds his hip like a scroll

yet he does not let me go

jennifer pirecki

you would thrive
unfolding
beneath her warmth

anthroprose

she saw your promise
yet unformed

jennifer pirecki

he taught me his craft
I lacked skill
and want for it

anthroprose

I wish to tell him
of my gratitude
he knew who I was
and was kind
in his care for me

if not for him
there would be
no Way

it was not easy for him

jennifer pirecki

      the choice
      the knowledge
      the depth
      the effort

      the loneliness

anthroprose

I know you
I lived you
I live you
I am you

jennifer pirecki

winds of doubt
buffet
your confusion

too difficult
to reason

you can reach me
with quiet
unseen efforts
in the stillness

jennifer pirecki

he would pull from
something deeper within
for the home stretch
would test
would try
would deplete

this is what Water told me

sacrifice
friendship
success
oppression
loneliness
alienation
rejection
defeat
betrayal
fear unto trembling
grief
despair
celebration
death
triumph

experience it all
nothing withheld

jennifer pirecki

experience it all
nothing withheld

at times
when quiet
overtakes me

I listen

jennifer pirecki

       read between these lines
       know
       that I know
       and think of him

anthroprose

this
the beginning
of courage
and preparation

jennifer pirecki

>there is no way
>around
>his travail
>only through

those days
are behind me now
scarred over
and dry

jennifer pirecki

I have taken up
my husband's children
fed them
cleaned them
loved them
to no avail

all I have known
is their contempt

anthroprose

has not a shred of your living death stayed with you?

jennifer pirecki

you
understand little
to nothing
your bitterness blinds
you

anthroprose

what is this anger?

jennifer pirecki

did your vow
mean nothing?

am I to answer
to the whims
of your entitlement?

anthroprose

do you seek
more than
your very life?

jennifer pirecki

what are your designs?

do you think
my love should be
withheld?

jennifer pirecki

your part
somehow insufficient
for your agenda

anthroprose

the constant foreboding is enough

jennifer pirecki

      his earthly end
      kept from me
      this is grace
      too much
      to bear

anthroprose

in many ways
we are each other's

jennifer pirecki

I can see
sadness emerging
from what is required

he carries this
with solidity

it was early
that I learned
to contain my anxiety

I have tried

jennifer pirecki

> our fractures
> might shatter us all
> with any more strain

anthroprose

I fear
you will not remember
the truth
of my unfailing kindness

jennifer pirecki

a mother's love
holds endless yearnings
for a family
never meant to be

doesn't
every wedding celebration
hold an opportunity
for drama?

jennifer pirecki

it takes every bit of effort not to cling

how are you?
is something wrong?
is it me?
what can I do?

jennifer pirecki

> I dream
> of that day
> even now

his eyes meet mine
he knows
before I utter words

jennifer pirecki

living this frail existence
cultivated seeds of knowing
like no amount of study
ever could

while depleted
I hear the centering Truth
in my own voice
it invigorates me
feeling once again
to my core
I Am

jennifer pirecki

reduce me
to a version
to satisfy

anthroprose

where is the hole big enough for my retreat?

jennifer pirecki

    I wonder
what they think of me
my parents long gone now

my mind's eye sees
her womb closing
no longer
a leaky cistern

jennifer pirecki

he waited in hope
to hear from Me

I chose My timing
carefully

anthroprose

I care not what they think

jennifer pirecki

what was
once precious
has become sullied

my burning fire
is stoked by it

cleanse
purify

their darkness
is ravenous
it will consume

not while I am on watch

jennifer pirecki

those
who travel with me
still grapple
with the effort
the dedication
the devotion

they waiver in holding fast

it is not my path
to sit idly by

I am brazen in this way

jennifer pirecki

you see
all I have
is this fervor

to come here
to the terrain
of their schemes
their thievery

it provokes them
but time is short

jennifer pirecki

> I am pressed
> by time
> by vultures
> ready to devour

let them
sleepwalk
through
their
living
death

jennifer pirecki

in blindness
I see
the folly
the gravity

how
he did not strike me down
his grace

remain on the Way
as I make sense of it

dreams persist
I have grown accustomed
to hearing from you that way

without them
I would have fled
long ago

jennifer pirecki

he called this Love
this foreign current
and I dreaded its surfacing
and focusing on me

let my dark corners be
is that too much to ask?

life is fleeting
vaporous
here for a moment
an inkling of Time
a butterfly on the wind

jennifer pirecki

to be seen
you must see
to be known
you must know

this takes time
from your Time
so make haste
do not delay

pot-stirrer
heralding the news
the message:
my food
my drink
my sustenance

One was coming

jennifer pirecki

    like wheat
    that blows
    in the summer wind
    we wait to be cut down
    milled
    served

doubt
sneaks in
nibbling at the edges
of my resolve
my clarity
my memory

jennifer pirecki

a flicker of excitement
caught somewhere
in my soul
as he unfurled his ideas

to this day
I know not why
he selected me

I quickened
their departure
late was my arrival
they had little left
so
they let me go

jennifer pirecki

my wilderness homeland
taught me
to channel my energy
which exhausted my parents

anthroprose

ready to initiate
that was my role
that was my singular focus

jennifer pirecki

      scrape as I have
      there is nothing
      used up and hollow
      like chaff to be blown
      by the summer wind

the only way
I know he is True
he knows everything about me
about them all
about the one I love
but keep hidden

jennifer pirecki

> at first
> I try to shrug him off
> all are repulsed by me
> unclean
> of
> the
> unclean

she refuses to look at me
avoids my gaze
urges me
to move along
she suffered
at the hands
of her husbands

she is wary
understandably so

jennifer pirecki

　

I know her secrets
I know about him
I know about the little ones lost

I see the brightness

there has been much
placed between us
none of that matters
hear me?

your Person
my pipeline

jennifer pirecki

choose
surrender
acceptance

receive
joy

can't you see
I just want some quiet?
some respite?
some peace?
some time to myself
that isn't fraught
with this turmoil?

jennifer pirecki

my needling attempts
remind him of his mother
no overcoming that

anthroprose

her eyes would narrow
focused on some horizon beyond
motivated by some knowledge
she held
but never shared

I would beg her to tell me

jennifer pirecki

blood curdling was his fury

anthroprose

I was the puny afterbirth
my hunger
never satisfied

jennifer pirecki

my schemes
have run out
no help
no guidance
just silence
and dread
and now
this fight

force of spirit
can misdirect

suffering
often comes
with lonely solitude
while strangers
share unexpectedly

resolving
what is unfinished
within one's Self
requires great fortitude

numerous lessons
I have learned

jennifer pirecki

>
> in those dire moments
> when your end is in view
> and you cannot see
> your strength
> for the desperate grasping
> and clinging
> to the life you know
> a release will come
> for having emptied yourself

anthroprose

pouring out
does not remove
capacity for fullness
it is the beginning
of fullness

jennifer pirecki

step-by-step
I carry my own burden

he winces
from pain unspeakable
yet
he does not let me go

jennifer pirecki

      she
      is too old
      to fight
      the sideways looks

      they only
      serve to strengthen
      how she sees herself
      how she has felt
      for as long
      as she can remember

anthroprose

sorrow
has etched its way
into the corners
of her downward smile

she is lost to herself

jennifer pirecki

> I mean to share
> with her
> she will be the first
> to know fully
>
> what will she do?

another
day
lost
to
mundane
movements

jennifer pirecki

I leave nothing
but a legacy
of barrenness
that is my lot

I know her secrets
she does not know mine
but I have them
how I struggled
to find my way

we have more in common
than she imagines

jennifer pirecki

I see her
I know her
I even understand her
heart hardened
like her clay jug

she must
catch a glimpse

she drinks with them
to dull the pain
of the cracks

but she will soften
just enough
to see her worth

jennifer pirecki

my deepest knowing:
I am grateful
to be unencumbered
salvaging pockets
of daily freedoms
for myself

gathering remnants
of my dignity
stitched together

somehow
he causes me to feel
comfortable enough
to banter about
this living water

he has me curious

jennifer pirecki

I spend my days
wondering
what more there must be
most people tire of me

he is the first
to take me seriously

my Path
is beyond
their prejudice

jennifer pirecki

what forbearance
what
strength of character

she has
suffered
in the hidden shadows
of her existence

I wish
she could see
the One
who brings
light and life
and all she longs for
within herself

jennifer pirecki

I am
grateful
for the Waters
that quench thirst

my voice
speaks for me
in a way
I could have never imagined

who am I?

jennifer pirecki

your wayward dysfunction
unchecked
invokes the veil

such painful silence
is not My absence
although it may feel
that way

would
that I would be
reclining against
my father's olive trees
than this withering vine
in a barren wilderness

what is my reward for sacrificing?

jennifer pirecki

you show
those wretches
your mercy
but none remains
for me

anthroprose

were my days
in the belly of the beast
a trifle?

jennifer pirecki

you want him
to grasp the greatness

you believe he can

anthroprose

live in constant surrender to the Beyond

jennifer pirecki

like quicksand
your favor is fickle

anthroprose

I was unseen
but with him
in the belly
of the great fish

jennifer pirecki

who lives through their body's own decomposition?

he was
the only one to
vigorously proclaim
the Message

jennifer pirecki

lost souls
found
prodigals
return

I blinked
it was over
irretrievable

jennifer pirecki

> I will wait
> I will be patient
> I want no less
> than to learn
> I am not easily fooled

anthroprose

to flourish
is to cultivate
to nurture
to know
intimately

jennifer pirecki

the vision
to see
beauty in wisdom
color in fruit

the space
and time
to linger
for the One

anthroprose

this
gnawing restlessness
a shade lighter
than my discontent

jennifer pirecki

whatever preceded
this fateful choice
my longings?
my loneliness?

both
all

I am
the queen
of looking back
presently
a pile of salt

jennifer pirecki

Timing
has meaning
beyond imagining

anthroprose

my remaining hope
has waned
burnt itself out

jennifer pirecki

I forget to remember
I remember to forget
I find my vision
only to lose it
I fight to know
only to not know

I carry
his sign
a testament
to his nights
of howling desperation
only to hear silence

jennifer pirecki

the need
for relief
is survival
is preservation

this
his elder season
he is alone

jennifer pirecki

    it is true
    the Way
    is narrow

I dream of that day
even now

a seamless interlude
of dance-like movements
my arms become branches
that lower His head
until it is immersed
in the flow

jennifer pirecki

    this dream of a memory
    is all I have left
    it is all that remains

    I wish I could hold on to it
    in this forsaken place
    where there is no comfort

the race
had begun long before
He trained for it well

living through
would deplete His reserves

jennifer pirecki

He would pull
from something deeper
to endure

this was only His beginning

His passing through
the symbolic waters
of death to life
was His clear acceptance
of the mission

I could hardly
contain My relief

jennifer pirecki

kindred
you have done well
to fulfill your part

I await your arrival

anthroprose

He would have never asked
for My validation

I knew
the desert sifting
was to come

this declaration
was meant
to sustain him

jennifer pirecki

I listen
for Voice
He boomed
unmistakable
that day

anthroprose

I return home
following
the desert wandering
eager to share
what else I have learned
about my Self
with those I love most

jennifer pirecki

my body moves
before thoughts can form
I understand
how this is to be solved

anthroprose

I have no fight
nothing to spend
but my humiliation
my infirmity
veils all
but my next step

jennifer pirecki

I was strong and loyal
my brooding would morph
into confidence
under his nurture

anthroprose

he was sure
to call me
on my short sightedness
caring enough
to be firm with me
and keep me
from hindering his path

jennifer pirecki

      somehow
      he saw fit to rename me
      somehow
      I know not how
      I became his rock
      and we became friends

you were never meant
to carry the yoke
that was mine only
to bear

jennifer pirecki

I wonder
how I ever contributed
my success too often
one step from defeat

there were moments
I thought I knew better
how could I?

I left that wilderness
for yet another
inhospitable
in every way

jennifer pirecki

from my earliest reckoning
I had hoped for a friend
to travel with me

I am Beautiful
as you are

jennifer pirecki

your end
remains a mystery
even in this
we are one

anthroprose

you no longer fight
the tide of your calling

reap the benefits of miracles

jennifer pirecki

what was once
stubborn in you
is now relentless fervor
for me

anthroprose

friend
I will meet you there
at another gate
the place
I told you about
so many times

jennifer pirecki

> even
> in your denial
> or your slumber
> I was with you

words flow
like honey
from the comb
complete with bee's sting
leaving its welt
again and again

jennifer pirecki

I know
the inside
of every prison

jails cannot hold me

that I was absentee
still nags at my conscience
my regret
my constant companion

jennifer pirecki

    he
    had his end in sight
    so it seemed
    he
    knew all along
    what would happen

    this remained with me

lost
to their carelessness
they are bound
to tire of me
soon

jennifer pirecki

what is my reward
for sacrificing these years?
this
is exactly why I ran

You have no care for me
it would have been better
for me to perish

jennifer pirecki

you cannot be unaware
of what these have perpetrated

I knew You would preserve them

anthroprose

his eyes are weak
mired in regret
spent beyond resources
he now wants rest

jennifer pirecki

>
> my studies
> revealed me to my Self
> a welcome relief
> from my younger years
> filled with hunger
> for my true Origins

the arc of my forefather's journey
yielded an important discovery:

my people
could not retain
Truth

jennifer pirecki

I can sympathize now
it is effort
to stay clear and connected
to Unwavering Love
for my Self
and my Purposes
when there is rejection

and there is always that

I remember the words
of an ancient forebear:

a prophet has no honor
in his hometown

jennifer pirecki

what you
cannot see
I see you

your blessed injury
plays its part
releasing your fight
your flight

you contend
with your unsteady gait

jennifer pirecki

I am not to extinguish
but redirect him
while experiencing
the bounds of his power

anthroprose

sacred
shifts
painful
breakages

jennifer pirecki

birthing
God-in-the-flesh-of-my-son
brought many fears
wrought an insatiable appetite

how can I not
turn towards him
for anything?
everything?

my intuition
a heavy burden
I have smothered him
with protection

jennifer pirecki

it is agonizing
to release him
to his fate
much less share
him with Him

her love stifled me
a traumatic entry
would seal our earthly bond

I am equipped
for my end
as she was
for my beginnings

jennifer pirecki

consider
a new way
of being
and believing

anthroprose

this
insufficient tribute
to the Man
my essential Hero

jennifer pirecki

    to finish the gauntlet
    requires both
    courage
    and
    surrender

my last moments
reveal that
I Am Sent
if only
for this friend

we walk this path
together

jennifer pirecki

may these
serve as light
illuminating
the Beyond
within

anthroprose

you see
this is
all yours
to accept

jennifer pirecki

what is at stake?

I am

I would rather be the vessel
than the water or the wine

cast by the Craftsman
forged by the Flame
I am used
reused

grounding portal
conduit of Grace
channel of sustenance
these my charge

I hold the Unknowable Fullness
for the season that is mine
Its weight and weather
Its need to expand

I may crack
I may chip
but I am emptied
I am filled
and I am not consumed

—what the vessel knows

acknowledgments

I remain grateful to those who have contributed to this volume in innumerable ways yet may not be mentioned here. These especially include readers with whom I have had the privilege of corresponding since the release of *Reckoning With Dust*.

To Bekah Doran, aside from your cherished friendship, your guidance was pivotal in both inspiring and providing shape to what this project has become. Abundant thanks.

To Bailey Rushlow, deep gratitude for helping me discover my bearings in foreign terrain which enabled the life of this work to be a flourishing one.

To Julie Godfrey, heartfelt appreciation for your kindred spirit rich with meaningful support. You are a beacon of light to all you encounter.

To Sandi Rice, your friendship and advocacy to keep creatively generating that which I am meant to consistently spurs me onward.

To Monty Powell, my on-call creative confidante, thank you for celebrating with me and sharing your wisdom.

To Scott Norton, your expertise and wise prompting, always delivered in love, without fail, continues to uplift my creative spirit.

To Zoya, for whatever life holds, may you be encouraged by the words within these pages.

As always, to my beloved Bruno, and to our Totem, what it means to me to be traveling with you on this journey remains beyond words.

To my Source and the Anthropos who serves as inspiration for this work, what a humbling honor to bring forth that which You give generously.

about anthroprose

Once an initial excerpt from *Reckoning With Dust* posted across several social media platforms, it became evident that highlighting its poetic verses rendered its ancient wisdom accessible for daily contemplation.

Anthroprose is the result of that discovery, and is infused with hope that it may provide daily encouragement for your Life's journey.

about the author

In 2017, Jennifer Pirecki published her debut collection, *Reckoning With Dust,* which pays tribute to the resilience of our human nature as expressed through her contemporary look at the human journey of Jesus and his fellow travelers.

Anthroprose, Reckoning's literary sibling, was chiefly inspired by her postings and correspondence across various social media platforms.

Jennifer is a speaker, educator and psychotherapist in private practice serving the greater Nashville area. She resides in Franklin, Tennessee, with her husband, Bruno, and their ridiculously spoiled Rhodesian Ridgeback, Totem.

www.jenniferpirecki.com
IG: @ jennifer.pirecki
FB: jennifer pirecki author

Made in the USA
Lexington, KY
19 November 2018